THIS BOOK BELONGS TO THE ULTIMATE BRAINROT BADDIE

____

Published by
GRAPEVINE BOOKS

www.grapevinebooks.com
Delhi | Mumbai
email: contact@grapevinebooks.com

Ordering Information:
Quantity sales: Special discounts are available on quantity purchases by corporations, associations, and others.
For details, reach out to the publisher.

First published by Grapevine Books 2025

ABOUT THIS BOOK

Welcome to the World of Italian Brainrot!

Ever felt your brain spin in chaotic circles after watching those wild Italian Brainrot memes? Good. That means you're in the right place. This book is your ticket to the bizarre, hilarious, and endlessly creative world of Italian Brainrot: a place where memes collide, chaos reigns, and colors bring the madness to life.

WHAT'S INSIDE?

Coloring Pages
Meme Lore
Guess the Meme
Mini-Games

PENTUNG
POS RONDA

WiFi
Signal

5x3=15
3/X=
X=?

Z
Z

G

PENTUNG
POS ROND

GUESS THE MEME

Your answer:

____

Your answer:

____

GUESS THE MEME

Your answer:

Your answer:

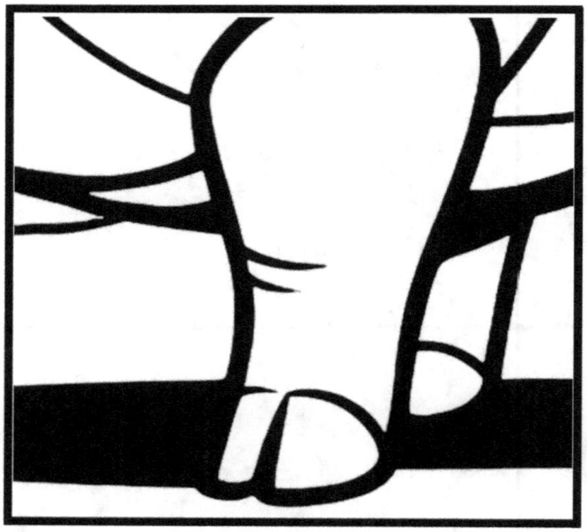

GUESS THE MEME

Your answer:

Your answer:

GUESS THE MEME

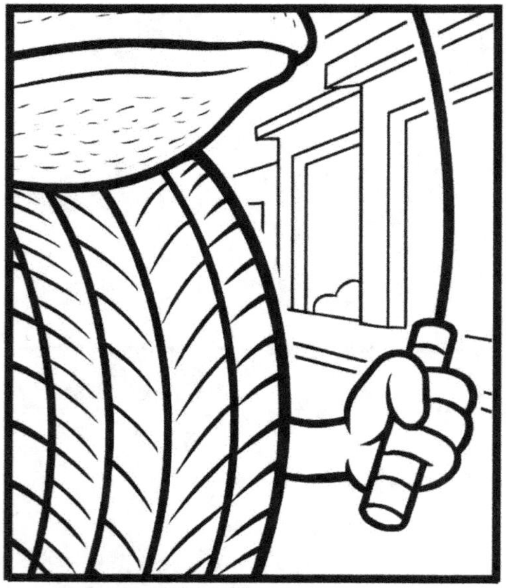

Your answer:

Your answer:

GUESS THE MEME

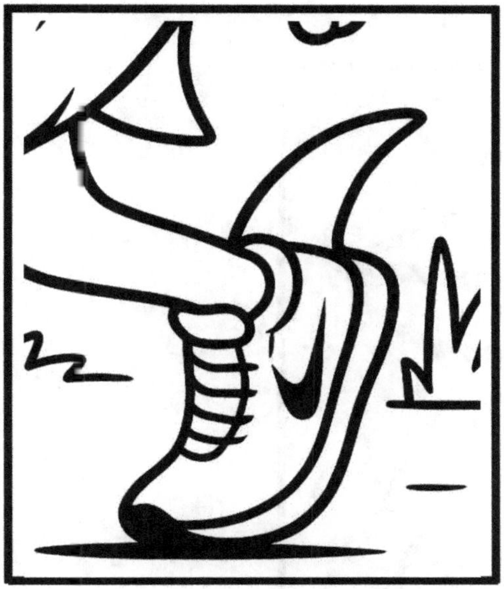

Your answer:

Your answer:

GUESS THE MEME

Your answer: ______________________

CONNECT THE DOTS

CONNECT THE DOTS

CONNECT THE DOTS

FiND THE DiFFERENCES

Hint: There are 5 differences

FIND THE DIFFERENCES

Hint: There are 5 differences

FiND THE DiFFERENCES

Hint: There are 5 differences

FiND THE DiFFERENCES

Hint: There are 5 differences

FiND THE DiFFERENCES

Hint: There are 5 differences

www.ingramcontent.com/pod-product-compliance
Lightning Source LLC
LaVergne TN
LVHW080551090726
842905LV00033B/658

* 9 7 8 9 3 6 3 1 1 3 3 8 1 *